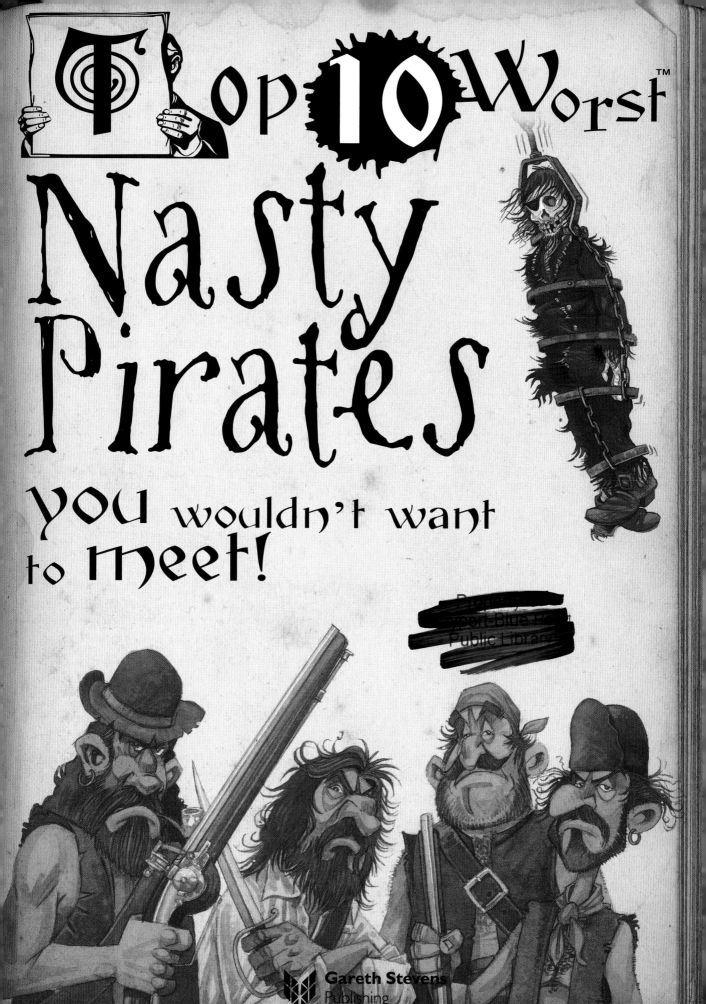

Please visit our Web site, **www.garethstevens.com**. For a free color catalog of all our high-quality books, call toll free 1-800-542-2595 or fax 1-877-542-2596.

Library of Congress Cataloging-in-Publication Data

Macdonald, Fiona.
Nasty pirates / Fiona Macdonald.
     p. cm. — (Top 10 worst)
Includes bibliographical references and index.
ISBN 978-1-4339-4086-6 (pbk. : alk. paper)
ISBN 978-1-4339-4087-3 (6-pack)
ISBN 978-1-4339-4085-9 (library binding : alk. paper)
1. Pirates-Juvenile literature. I. Title.
G535.M216 2011
364.16'4-dc22

2010004121

First Edition

Published in 2011 by
Gareth Stevens Publishing
111 East 14th Street, Suite 349
New York, NY 10003

© 2010 The Salariya Book Company Ltd

Series creator: David Salariya
Editor: Stephen Haynes
Illustrations by David Antram

Printed in Heshan, China

CPSIA compliance information: Batch #SS10GS: For further information contact Gareth Stevens, New York, New York at 1-800-542-2595.

Top 10 Worst

Nasty Pirates

you wouldn't want to meet!

Illustrated by
David Antram

Written by
fiona Macdonald

Created & designed by
David Salariya

Contents

Pirates everywhere!

Ahoy there! Join this book's voyage of exploration to find the world's Top 10 Worst Nasty Pirates. Bold, brave, and adventurous, pirates were exciting heroes. However, these glamorous raiders were also brutal robbers and bloodthirsty mass murderers. At different times, and in different places, they were known by many different names:

Sea-Wolf (Viking)

Пират or Pirat (Russian)

Corsair (french)

Vrijbuiter (Dutch)

Call me what ye please, I'm still a raider o' the seas!

Buccaneer (Caribbean)

Hai dao (Chinese)

Pirate (English)

Woku (Japanese)

Heroes or villains?

Sailing! Robbing! Fighting! Pirate life was brutal and bloodstained. Why did men—and women—choose such a risky career? Many were criminals or adventurers. For them, the sea was a place to hide, or find freedom. Some were traders and explorers; a few were holy warriors. Most important of all, pirates wanted treasure. Stolen gold could make an ordinary crewman as rich as a king.

Swashbuckling pirates

Yo ho ho! Most of us have enjoyed exciting pirate movies, set in exotic locations and featuring handsome heroes. Pirates in books and movies are brave, romantic, and glamorous. They fight for noble causes. They are heroes—and nothing like real pirates who lived long ago!

All aboard, you scurvy dogs!

Ahoy there!

6

Explorers

It cost a fortune to buy a fine ship, so many explorers raised money for their epic voyages by piracy. English hero Sir Francis Drake led the second voyage ever around the world (from 1577 to 1581), and raided Spanish ships and settlements in South America and the Caribbean.

Privateers

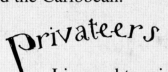

Licensed to raid—and to kill! Privateers were raiders with written permission from kings, queens, and other powerful people to attack ships belonging to enemies. Some privateers, like French admiral René Duguay-Trouin (1673–1736), combined privateering with brilliant careers in national navies. He captured 300 merchant vessels as a privateer—plus 20 enemy warships—for France.

Privateer and Scholar

English privateer William Dampier (1651–1715) made three voyages to Asia and Australia and filled notebooks with wonderful descriptions of the people, animals, and plants he observed there. He made notes of winds and tides, drew maps, collected specimens, and caused a sensation by bringing tattooed slaves home with him to London.

Jean Lafitte

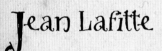

What treasures did pirates most hope to capture? Gold, jewels, guns, ships—and slaves from Africa. Caribbean-born* Jean Lafitte (c. 1776–1823) raided slave ships, sold slaves, and helped smugglers. He also set up a lawless "pirate kingdom" at Galveston, Texas.

Some say he was born in France, but this is less likely.

A world of danger

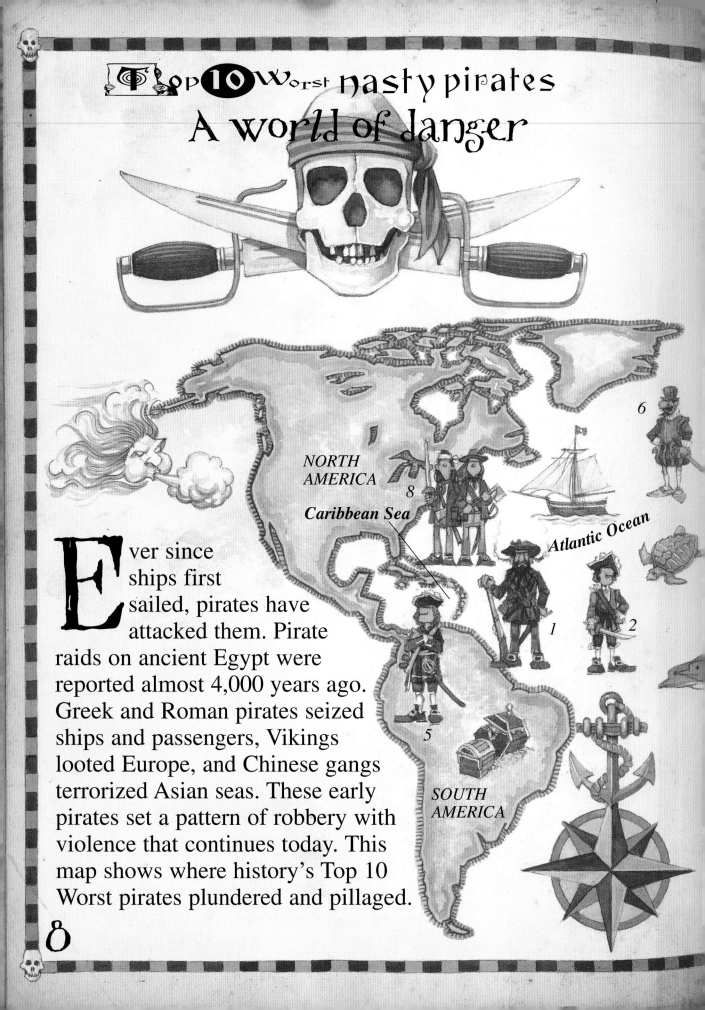

Ever since ships first sailed, pirates have attacked them. Pirate raids on ancient Egypt were reported almost 4,000 years ago. Greek and Roman pirates seized ships and passengers, Vikings looted Europe, and Chinese gangs terrorized Asian seas. These early pirates set a pattern of robbery with violence that continues today. This map shows where history's Top 10 Worst pirates plundered and pillaged.

NORTH AMERICA

Caribbean Sea

Atlantic Ocean

SOUTH AMERICA

1. *Blackbeard*
2. *Bartholomew Roberts*
3. *Zheng Yi Sao*
4. *Henry Avery*
5. *Sir Henry Morgan*
6. *Sir Francis Drake*
7. *Barbarossa brothers*
8. *Anne Bonny and Mary Read*
9. *Sweyn Asleifsson*
10. *Captain Kidd*

Pirates today

Today, piracy is increasing—fast. Danger zones include the seas off East Africa and Indonesia. Today's pirates are often poor and desperate. Their lives are threatened by climate change, global trade, and war. Other pirates work for criminal bosses and drug dealers. All are very dangerous.

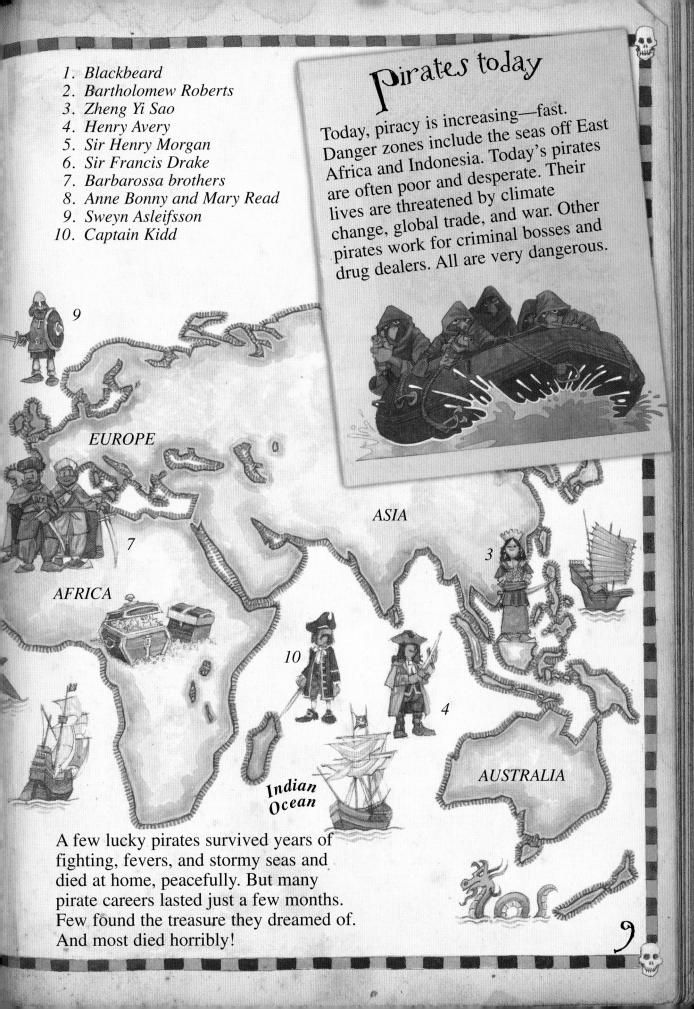

9

EUROPE

ASIA

7

AFRICA

3

10

4

Indian
Ocean

AUSTRALIA

A few lucky pirates survived years of fighting, fevers, and stormy seas and died at home, peacefully. But many pirate careers lasted just a few months. Few found the treasure they dreamed of. And most died horribly!

No 10

Captain Kidd

British privateer William Kidd was licensed to attack the French, and pirates. In 1698, he captured the magnificent *Quedah Merchant*. It flew a French flag, but came from India. Furious Indian princes accused Kidd of piracy, and the English agreed. Kidd's crew deserted him, and he sailed away to hide.

Vital Statistics

Name:	William Kidd
Nickname:	"Captain Kidd"
Lived:	1645 to 1701
Born:	Scotland
Career:	Privateer, pirate
Sailed:	Caribbean, Indian Ocean
Died:	Hanged

You wouldn't want to know this:

Kidd was hanged twice! The first time, the hangman's rope broke, and he survived. So they hanged him again!

Abandon ship!

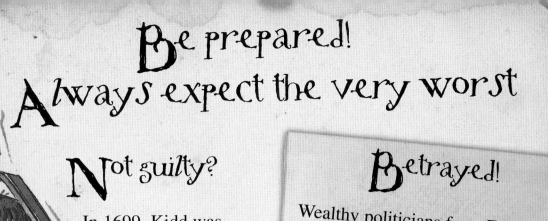

Be prepared!
Always expect the very worst

Not guilty?

In 1699, Kidd was captured in Boston and shipped to London, where he was sentenced to death for piracy. But was he really guilty?

Betrayed!

Wealthy politicians from England and Ireland had secretly financed Kidd's privateering voyage. In return, they expected a generous share of his booty. But when the English government put Kidd on trial, these backers disowned him to protect their own political careers. If they had spoken up for Kidd, he might have been pardoned and set free.

Buried treasure

After Kidd died, people wondered where he had buried his loot from the *Quedah Merchant*. Rumors said that it was hidden on Long Island, now part of New York. But treasure hunters have never found it!

Warning

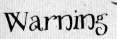

Kidd's body was coated in pitch (sticky, waterproof tar), put in an iron cage, and hung by the docks at Tilbury, near London. It gave a grisly greeting to sailors and pirates.

No 9

Sweyn Asleifsson

Good friends, a fertile farm, a big house and a fine family—Sweyn Asleifsson had everything! How did he get it? Mostly by fighting, looting, and killing! Sweyn was a typical Viking pirate. He fought to win fame and glory, to protect his family from bloody feuds, to win riches—and, according to Viking poets—because he enjoyed it.

Vital Statistics

Name: Sweyn Asleifsson
Lived: *c.* 1120 to 1160
Born: Orkney Islands (between Scotland and Norway
Career: Pirate and raider
Sailed: Scotland, Ireland, Wales
Died: Of natural causes, at home

You wouldn't want to know this:

Sweyn and Rosta were bitter Viking enemies. In 1139, Sweyn burned down Rosta's house, even though he knew that Rosta's family was trapped inside.

Raiders from the sea!

Yaarrgh!

In fine weather, Viking pirates raided peaceful coastal villages, monasteries, and markets. They sailed their fast, sleek dragon ships up onto a beach, then leaped out, brandishing sharp swords and brutal battle-axes. Terrified villagers hid or ran away. Raids were a bloody business; the Vikings showed no mercy!

Be prepared!
Always expect the very worst

Loot!

Viking pirates grabbed anything they could sell: gold and silver from churches, furs and amber from traders—and young men and women, to be used as slaves.

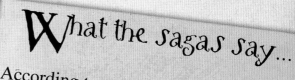

What the sagas say...

According to a poem called the *Orkneyinga Saga*, written in Iceland around AD 1200, Sweyn spent his year this way:

- Winter: at home with his warriors

- Early spring: planting crops on his farm

- Late spring: raiding Ireland and the Scottish Islands

- Summer: on his farm, harvesting crops

- Autumn: sailing on more pirate raids

Bloody love

In 1140, Sweyn sailed south, chasing pirates from Wales. Landing on the Isle of Man, he met a beautiful, sorrowful woman. Welsh pirates had just killed her husband. She agreed to marry Sweyn, but only after he had caught and killed all her husband's murderers.

Sweyn boasted that he could entertain 80 warriors for a whole winter. They passed the dark Orkney days and nights in his great hall, eating, drinking, and telling stories of their adventures.

13

No 8

Anne Bonny and Mary Read

Women are trouble! That's what pirate captains said, and most sailors agreed with them. They complained that females brought bad luck, or made crewmen jealous and quarrelsome. Everyone knew that women could not fight or sail a ship—and everyone was amazed when two particularly cruel, clever pirates turned out to be women! Their names were Anne Bonny and Mary Read.

Vital Statistics

Name:	Anne Bonny
Born:	County Cork, Ireland
Career:	Pirate
Lived:	c. 1697 (some say 1682) to 1721 (some say 1782!)
Sailed:	Caribbean
Died:	Unknown

Name:	Mary Read
Born:	Plymouth, England
Career:	Pirate
Lived:	c. 1690 to 1721
Sailed:	Caribbean
Died:	Of fever, in jail

Sharing tasks with sailors

It's not all plunder and treasure, you know.

To stay safe on board ship, Anne and Mary hid the fact that they were women from all the other sailors. Bloodthirsty, brave, and extremely tough, they worked as hard as all the men, and were famous for their "unladylike" fierceness, swearing, and bad tempers.

Be prepared!
Always expect the very worst

Runaway couple

Anne Cormac emigrated from Ireland to America. There, she married James Bonny, a failed pirate (and a spy), but she was unhappy. She fell in love with another pirate, "Calico Jack" Rackham, and ran away with him. Together, they cruised the Caribbean, plundering ships and taking prisoners— including Mary Read—to sell as slaves.

Always in disguise

Young Mary Read worked as a page and a ship's cabin boy, to earn money for her mother. Still dressed in male clothes, she joined the English army, married a soldier, and helped him run an inn. After he died, Mary went back to sea, was captured by Calico Jack, and became a pirate.

Calico Jack

Nicknamed "Calico Jack" for the fine cotton shirts he wore, Rackham was much less brave than Read or Bonny. He refused to fight when the British navy attacked his ship, and was arrested and found guilty. Bonny was scornful:

If you had fought like a man you needn't have hang'd like a dog.

15

No 7

Henry Avery

A lifelong sailor, Henry Avery went to sea as a boy on English navy ships. Seeking quick riches, he became a slave trader in West Africa, enslaving the merchants who sold slaves to him. Popular, and a born leader, he became a pirate after leading a mutiny against an English captain. Then he headed far east, and had amazing luck! He captured the Mughal emperor's ship, *Ganj-i-Sawai*, laden with fabulous treasures.

Vital Statistics

Name:	Henry Avery (or Every)
Nickname:	"Long Ben"
Lived:	*c.* 1653 to *c.* 1699
Born:	Devon, England
Career:	Pirate
Sailed:	Indian Ocean
Died:	Fate unknown

You wouldn't want to know this:

There were hundreds of women on board the Mughal treasure ship. Many killed themselves, rather than be attacked by Avery's pirates.

Whack!

Be prepared!
Always expect the very worst

Deadly pirate weapons

Cutlass – *a sharp, broad-bladed butcher's knife. First used by buccaneers (see pages 18–19).*

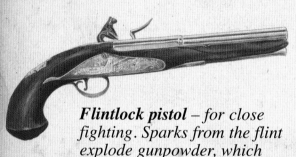

Bombs – *pots or bottles filled with a mixture of smoky explosives and killer lead shot.*

Flintlock pistol – *for close fighting. Sparks from the flint explode gunpowder, which shoots heavy lead balls.*

Chain-shot – *empty cannonball cases, joined by a chain, that cut through enemy ships' rigging.*

Death flag

Henry Avery may have been the first to fly the skull and crossbones flag. Sometimes called the "Jolly Roger," this was a sign that pirates would show no mercy. So was a plain red "*Jolie Rouge*" (pretty red) flag.

Each pirate captain had his own version of the Jolly Roger:

Christopher Moody   Blackbeard   Jack Rackham

Edward Low   Bartholomew Roberts   Thomas Tew

The greatest prize ever

The *Ganj-i-Sawai* was the richest prize ever captured by a pirate. A huge dhow (cargo ship) with valuable guns, she carried priceless pearls, precious stones, and half a million coins of solid gold and silver, as well as other treasures—including a saddle encrusted with real rubies!

No 6

Sir Henry Morgan

The Spanish Main was a very dangerous place. But young Henry Morgan went there, keen to win fame and fortune by fighting against Spain. He was sent on secret missions by the English to attack Spanish settlements, leading shiploads of savage buccaneers.

In 1671, he destroyed Panama, a peaceful Spanish city, and was sent home in disgrace. But England needed his skills and knowledge, so he was pardoned and ended his career as governor of Jamaica.

Vital Statistics

Name:	Sir Henry Morgan
Nickname:	"Captain Blood"
Lived:	c. 1635 to 1688
Born:	Wales
Career:	Buccaneer leader
Sailed:	Caribbean
Died:	Peacefully, from illness

You wouldn't want to know this:

When attacking Spanish settlements, Morgan used priests, nuns, and even children as human shields and hostages.

What are you looking at?

Buccaneers were runaway slaves, criminals, pirates, and outlaws. They lived rough lives on Hispaniola (now Haiti and the Dominican Republic) and dressed in homemade, smelly, blood-stained animal hides.

Be prepared! Always expect the very worst

Pirate punishments

- **Bilboes** – These iron hoops, fastened around your ankles, will trap you on deck.

- **Cat-o'-nine-tails** – This whip has nine strands ("tails") studded with knots or fishhooks. It can kill.

- **Ducking** – You'll be tied to a rope and dipped into the sea. You might drown!

- **Keelhauling** – You'll be thrown overboard and dragged under the keel. It's covered with barnacles; they'll skin you alive— and you'll die!

One punishment you'll avoid is "walking the plank," or being forced along a strip of wood and into the sea. This way of killing was probably dreamed up by later writers; real pirates didn't do it.

Cat-o'-nine-tails

How buccaneers got their name

When not at sea, the wild bunch on Hispaniola hunted pigs and cattle and sold meat, fat, and hides to passing ships. Local Arawak people taught them how to preserve the meat in a *boucan*—the French word for "smokehouse" (settlers came from many parts of Europe). Soon, the hunters had a nickname: *boucaniers* (smokers). In English, this became "buccaneers."

Fireship!

In 1669, Morgan's buccaneers made a daring attack at Maracaibo, Venezuela. They filled hollow logs with gunpowder, loaded them on an empty ship, sailed it close to the Spanish fleet—then lit the fuses!

19

№ 5

Sir francis Drake

Master mariner, royal favorite, and world explorer, Drake rose from humble origins to become England's national hero. Raised on a houseboat, he learned seafaring skills from his uncle, a ruthless slave trader. Proud nobles despised Drake, but his courage helped defeat the Spanish Armada in 1588. And his privateering exploits won fabulous riches.

Vital Statistics

Name: Francis Drake
Nickname: *El Draque* (the Dragon)
Born: Devon, England
Lived: *c.* 1540 to 1596
Career: Explorer, slave trader, privateer
Sailed: Spanish Main; Pacific Ocean, around the world
Died: Of dysentery, in the Caribbean

Spanish gold

Every year, Spanish galleons laden with gold and silver mined in South America sailed from Panama back home to Spain.

Golden ornaments from South America

You wouldn't want to know this:

On his around-the-world voyage, Drake quarreled with his second-in-command, and had him hanged. But the night before, Drake had him to dinner in a very friendly fashion— and that was after passing sentence!

In 1579, Francis Drake captured the Spanish galleon *Nuestra Señora de la Concepción* off Ecuador. It took four days to unload all her treasure. This included 50 pounds (23 kg) of pure gold, and 20 tons of silver!

Be prepared!
Always expect the very worst
Take care in the "Spanish Main"

Map of the Spanish Main

West Indies

Cuba

Hispaniola

Central America

The seas around Spanish settlements in South America were known as the Spanish Main. Pirates and privateers from many European countries prowled the seas there, eager to attack Spanish treasure ships.

Queen Elizabeth I of England took a secret interest in Drake's privateering adventures. Around 1570, she gave him "letters of marque"—written permission—to attack treasure ships from Spain.

When Drake returned to England in 1581 after his historic voyage around the world, he brought enough pirate treasure with him to repay all the English government's debts—and buy himself a splendid mansion. As a reward, Queen Elizabeth I made him a knight.

Navigation

Like all pirate captains, it was Drake's task to navigate his ship through unknown waters. To find its position out of sight of land, Drake measured time passing, the ship's speed, its compass bearing, and the height of the sun. He then plotted (recorded) this information in logbooks and on traverse boards.

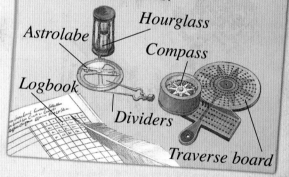

Hourglass

Astrolabe

Compass

Logbook

Dividers

Traverse board

Arise, Sir francis!

21

No 4

The Barbarossa Brothers

The Barbary Coast of North Africa was home to a rich, elegant Muslim civilization. But most Europeans did not know or care. They simply feared Barbary pirates! The most famous and successful, Aruj and Khayr ad-Din Barbarossa, won wars against Christian Spain, conquered kingdoms for Turkey, and helped thousands of Muslim refugees escape to safety. Khayr ad-Din also commanded the Turkish navy.

Barbary pirates sailed in galleys—warships rowed by slaves. Galley slaves were convicted criminals, or pirates' captives. Their lives were terrible. Chained to their seats, they were whipped to make them row faster.

Vital Statistics

Name:	Aruj
Nickname:	"Barbarossa" (Red Beard)
Lived:	1473 to 1518
Born:	Greece
Career:	Pirate
Sailed:	Mediterranean Sea
Died:	Executed by the Spanish
Name:	Khayr ad-Din
Nickname:	"Barbarossa" (Red Beard—he dyed it to copy his brother)
Lived:	c. 1475 to 1546
Born:	Greece
Career:	Pirate, Ottoman (Turkish) admiral
Sailed:	Mediterranean Sea
Died:	Of old age

You wouldn't want to know this:

In just one year, 1544, Khayr ad-Din Barbarossa captured 9,000 Christians and sold them as slaves.

The fight against Barbary pirates was led by corsairs (privateers) from Malta. Commanded by Christian knights, they fought against Islam, but were also keen to capture Muslim ships' valuable cargoes.

Be prepared!
Always expect the very worst

How to avoid Barbary pirates

- If you're traveling to the holy city of Jerusalem, go overland if possible. It takes longer than by sea, but it's safer.

- If you have heavy cargoes to transport and must cross the Mediterranean Sea, make sure that your vessel is protected by soldiers and warships.

- Steer north if you can. The Barbary pirates live on the southern shores of the Mediterranean. It's easier for them to raid close to home.

Soldier of fortune

Sir Francis Verney (1584–1615) was an English gentleman who became a Muslim and lived in Algiers, North Africa. For 6 years, he grew rich as a Barbary pirate. But he was captured by Christians, sold as a slave, and died soon after.

Fighting at sea

Human muscle power plus special triangular sails made galleys fast and easy to steer, ideal for attacks on slower cargo ships.

Barbary pirate ships carried troops of janissaries (trained soldiers), ready to leap onto enemy ships and overpower the crew.

In battle, galleys rowed quickly towards sailing ships, smashing holes in their hulls and sinking them. Crews were forced to surrender—or leap overboard and drown.

No 3

Zheng Yi Sao

Young and beautiful, Shi Xianggu wed pirate captain Zheng Yi. He commanded the largest Chinese fleet of his time. With 800 junks, 1,000 smaller ships, and 75,000 sailors, it may have been the greatest pirate fleet ever.

When Zheng Yi died in a tropical storm, Shi took over his pirate empire—and his name. Everyone called her "Zheng Yi Sao" (Zheng Yi's Widow). Her ships raided the South China Seas, robbing, destroying, and demanding taxes. In 1810, the Chinese government pardoned Zheng Yi Sao for her crimes. She married her dead husband's adopted son and gave up piracy forever.

Vital Statistics

Name:	Shi Xianggu
Nickname:	"Zheng Yi Sao" (Zheng Yi's Widow)
Born:	South China
Lived:	1775 or 1785 to 1844
Career:	Pirate
Sailed:	China Seas
Died:	At home, of old age

You wouldn't want to know this:

If one of Zheng Yi Sao's crew left her ship without permission, his ear was cut off as punishment.

Keeping control

Get to work, NOW!

As a woman pirate, Zheng Yi Sao had to be tougher than any man. She was famous for harsh punishments handed out to pirates who disobeyed her.

Be prepared!
Always expect the very worst

For fighting on board enemy ships, Chinese pirates chose long, heavy swords. They were so sharp that they could slice through metal.

Chinese pirates sailed in converted junks (cargo vessels). Fast, seaworthy, armed with cannons, and with big holds to store gunpowder, junks were ideal for fighting.

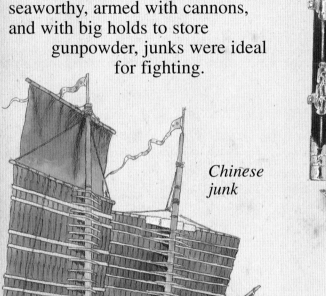

Chinese junk

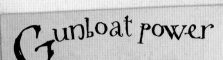

Gunboat power

To protect its profitable opium trade, the British government sent Royal Navy gunboats to attack Chinese pirates. In 1849, soon after Zheng Yi Sao died, they destroyed Chinese pirates' power forever by blowing up their ships at the mouth of the Haiphong River (now in Vietnam).

Doubly successful

After Zheng Yi Sao retired from pirate raiding, she began a second moneymaking career. She ran a gambling house in Guangzhou, and died a very rich woman!

No 2

Bartholomew Roberts

Famous for wanting "a short life and a merry one," Roberts was one of the most successful pirates ever. In just 2 years, he captured 400 ships, winning "pleasure, liberty, and power." In spite of his brilliant—and cruel—career, Roberts did not plan to be a pirate. Originally third mate on a slave-trading ship, he was chosen as captain when its crew mutinied. Today he is remembered for the remarkable rules he created for pirates to follow.

Looking this good is hard work.

Vital statistics

Name:	John (later Bartholomew) Roberts
Nickname:	"Black Bart"
Born:	Wales
Lived:	1682 to 1722
Career:	Pirate, slave trader
Sailed:	Brazil, Newfoundland (Canada), Caribbean, West Africa
Died:	In battle

You wouldn't want to know this:

Roberts caused such fear that for a year (1720–1721) few ships dared sail in Caribbean waters.

Dressed to kill

Roberts always put on his best clothes before battle: a velvet suit and a shirt trimmed with lace. Proud of his captain's rank, he wanted to encourage his men—and face death looking good.

Be prepared!
Always expect the very worst

Captain Roberts' rules

1. Fair shares of food and drink for all—and an equal vote on important decisions.

2. Equal shares of plunder for all crew.

3. Cheats to be marooned; onboard robbers to have noses and ears slit.

4. No gambling, dice, or cards.

5. Early to bed—no candles below decks.

6. No wives or girlfriends on voyages.

7. People caught deserting ship to be punished by death or marooning.

8. No fights or duels among crewmen at sea.

9. Wounded pirates to get a pension.

10. Ship musicians to have rest on Sundays.

How to fire a cannon

1. Ram gunpowder into the barrel.

2. Add wad (a woolen pad) to keep gunpowder in position.

3. Add cannonball.

4. Secure cannonball with wad.

5. Light the gunpowder with a match. It will explode and hurl the cannonball toward your enemies!

Barrel

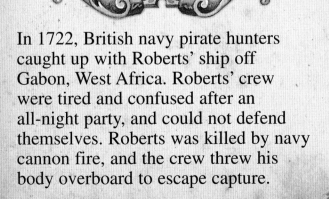

In 1722, British navy pirate hunters caught up with Roberts' ship off Gabon, West Africa. Roberts' crew were tired and confused after an all-night party, and could not defend themselves. Roberts was killed by navy cannon fire, and the crew threw his body overboard to escape capture.

No 1

Blackbeard

Most pirates were murderers, but Blackbeard chose a different way to win treasure, behaving like a madman to terrify sailors. This, plus the 40 cannons on his ship, forced victims to surrender. Blackbeard captured a rival pirate fleet, took control of Charleston port (now in South Carolina), then began new adventures. British Navy ships cornered him. He endured 5 gunshot wounds and 20 sword wounds before collapsing.

Vital Statistics

Name: Edward Teach
Nickname: "Blackbeard"
Born: Bristol, England
Lived: *c*. 1680 to 1718
Career: Pirate
Sailed: Caribbean
How he died: In battle

You wouldn't want to know this:

Blackbeard's headless body is said to have swum seven times around his ship. Then it disappeared!

Before battle, Blackbeard fixed lighted gun fuses under his hat. They surrounded him with devilish smoke. He also carried six pistols, all loaded.

A Ladies' Man?

Daddy!

Did Blackbeard's striking looks and international fame make him attractive to women? Rumors said he had at least 14 wives. But perhaps he invented these stories to increase his reputation!

Gruesome guard

Blackbeard hid his treasure somewhere near Charleston—perhaps on a deserted island. Frightened sailors reported that he buried a murdered pirate on top of each treasure chest to scare robbers away.

Marooned!

To keep his treasure to himself, Blackbeard marooned his pirate crew on a lonely island. He left them with a day's supply of water, some brandy (as medicine), and a gun—to shoot themselves if they felt desperate! Unless marooned men found food and fresh water, they were doomed to die. Marooning was a popular way for pirate captains to punish mutineers or dispose of unwanted captives.

Marooned... I'm doomed!

Down below

Blackbeard tested new recruits to his crew by shutting them up in his ship's hold, full of smoke and fumes.

29

Glossary

Armada A large group of warships.

Astrolabe A navigation instrument used to measure the position of the sun above the horizon.

Barbary Coast An old name for the coast of North Africa.

Barnacles Marine crustaceans with rough, pointed shells.

Bilboes Iron hoops fitted around the ankles, used to imprison sailors on the open deck of a ship.

Booty Stolen goods.

Boucan (French) A small building used for smoking meat to preserve it.

Buccaneers Wild, lawless pirate gangs living on Caribbean islands.

Cabin boy A young boy working as a servant or trainee sailor on board ship.

Calico Lightweight cotton cloth.

Corsairs Licensed raiders in the Mediterranean Sea and North Atlantic Ocean.

Cutlass A sharp, broad-bladed knife, first used by buccaneers.

Dhow A cargo ship with three masts; a high, curving hull; and triangular sails. It was built to sail in the Indian Ocean.

Dividers A mathematical instrument used to measure distances on a map or a globe.

Dock A place where ships can be tied up next to dry land.

Feud A long-standing argument between two groups or families.

Galleon A large cargo ship, built for long-distance voyages. It had a deep hull, three masts, and large rectangular sails.

Galley A streamlined warship built to sail the Mediterranean Sea. It was usually powered by slaves rowing.

Hold A compartment in a ship's hull where cargo is stored.

Hull The body of a ship.

Janissaries Well-trained slave soldiers from the Ottoman Empire, based in Turkey.

Junk A cargo ship with a flat-bottomed hull and stiff sails. Sailed in the seas around China.

Keel The heavy "backbone" at the bottom of a ship's hull.

Lead shot Small lead balls, fired from guns.

Logbook A record of a ship's movements.

Marooned Left to die on a deserted island.

Mughal A Muslim dynasty that ruled an empire in India from 1526 to 1858.

Mutiny Rebellion by a ship's crew.

Opium A drug made from the seeds of the opium poppy.

Page A young boy working as a servant.

Pardoned Forgiven.

Pension Money paid to support people who are too old or ill to work.

Privateers Raiders licensed to attack at sea.

Refugees People who leave their homes to escape danger.

Rigging Ropes that support a ship's masts and sails.

Saga A long story.

Spanish Main The seas around Spanish-ruled land in South America and the Caribbean.

Third mate A junior officer on board ship.

Traverse board A wooden board with pegs and holes, used to record the course steered by a ship.

Index